D1825353

Fin▶Paw▶Hand

Published by A & C Black (Publishers) Limited,
35 Bedford Row,
London WC1R 4JH

Lanners, Edi
   Fin → paw → hand.
   1. Human evolution — Juvenile literature
   I. Title   II. Lanners, Ruth
   573.2   GN281

ISBN 0-7136-1922-8

Translated by Helen Davies
First published 1980, English edition
© 1977 Reich Verlag AG, Lucerne
© 1980 A & C Black (Publishers) Limited

Filmset by Keyspools Limited, Golborne, Lancs
Printed in Great Britain by Hollen St. Press Ltd, Slough, Berks.

Fin ▶ Paw ▶ Hand

Edi and Ruth Lanners

Adam & Charles Black·London

This is our class

There are twenty-six of us in our class. We are all about eleven and we live near the Lake of Zurich in Switzerland.

We began to wonder why our hands are made as they are. Then we realised that we would have to find out about the whole of our body since hands are just one part of it. We decided to concentrate on discovering where humans came from, and how long people have been living on earth.

The first thing we learned was that five hundred million years ago only plants and very simple animals lived on earth. They lived in the sea.

We decided to make a family tree of the human race. We collected pictures of animals from newspapers, stamps showing animals, and stuffed animals from the school museum service. To make an accurate family tree, we had to find out which animals appeared first and which came later.

Our Noah's Ark

Everything that lives on earth is related, like a big family. How closely are we related to each kind of animal?

We know that most people like dogs much more than they like toads. The way we feel about different animals *might* point to how closely we are related to them. This possibility gave us the idea for our first experiment.

Suppose Tom lives on an island with different sorts of animals. A volcano erupts, and lava covers the island. Like Noah in the Bible, we have to rescue as many inhabitants as we can. We don't have much time, so we have to save the animals that seem to us the most important.

We put the animals on a step ladder in the order we would rescue them. Tom is at the top, because we would rescue him first.

The order after Tom is: squirrel, marmot, shrew, turtle, lizard, newt, fish, sea urchin, snail.

Without realising it, we have saved first the mammals, then the reptiles, amphibians, and fish, and lastly the invertebrate animals. You can try this experiment with your friends by making copies of the ten animals you can see on page 5.

dragonfly

ape

lizard

bird

mouse

rabbit

turtle

frog

octopus

fish

5

mouse

starfish

newt

fish

beetle

fly

worm

centipede

dragonfly

pearly nautilus

sea urchin

hare

whale

oyster

horse

lizard

wood louse

bird

butterfly

spider

lobster

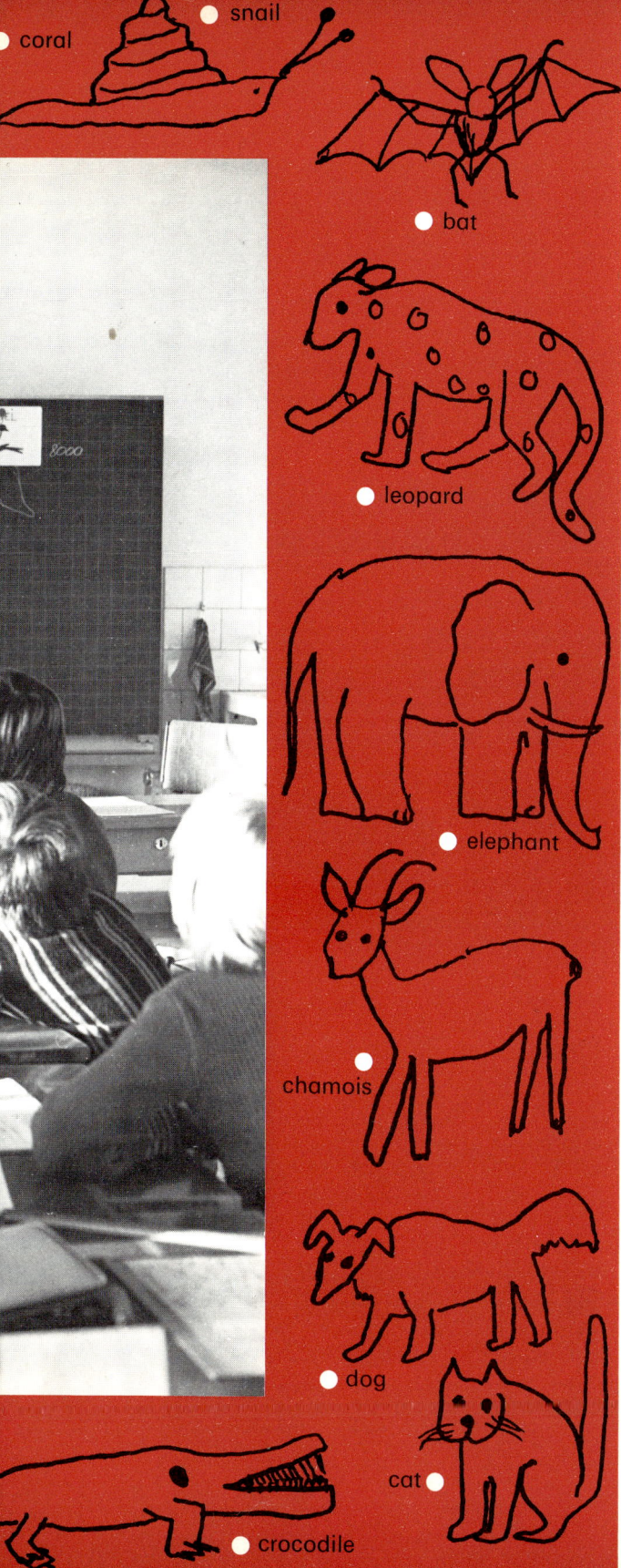

coral

snail

bat

leopard

elephant

chamois

dog

cat

crocodile

Animals without backbones

Well over a million different types of animal live on earth today. Countless others have become extinct. Most animals are very different from us. Those least like us are the animals without backbones. They are called invertebrate animals.

Invertebrates lived on the earth long before other kinds of animals appeared. The invertebrate group includes worms, snails, mussels, lobsters, spiders and insects. Their bodies are not supported by bones. Instead they are protected by a tough skin or shell.

The vertebrate group, which we belong to, is more complicated in design. All vertebrates have a backbone – the part of the skeleton which gives strong support for the body. The backbone is made up of bones called vertebrae, and this is why all animals with backbones are called vertebrates.

Because a skeleton with a backbone is able to carry a heavy load, vertebrates can become very big. Invertebrates never grow to an enormous size.

Can you find out which of the animals on these pages have backbones? You will find the answer on page 38.

All embryos look the same

You have seen that the vertebrate group contains some very different animals. But the tiny mouse and the huge elephant, the swift bird and the plodding tortoise are all related to each other. The vertebrates which live on land developed from fish millions of years ago.

How can we prove this? Look at the top row of pictures below. They show the tiny unborn young, or embryos, of various vertebrate animals. They look the same, but when their limbs develop they grow into quite different animals. In the row of pictures at the foot of pages 8 and 9 you can see how the embryos develop.

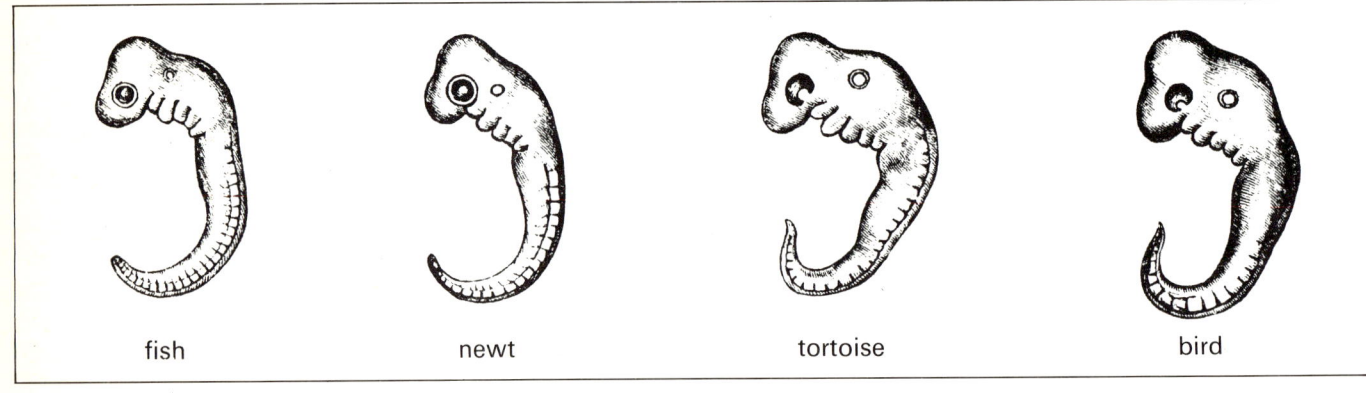

| fish | newt | tortoise | bird |

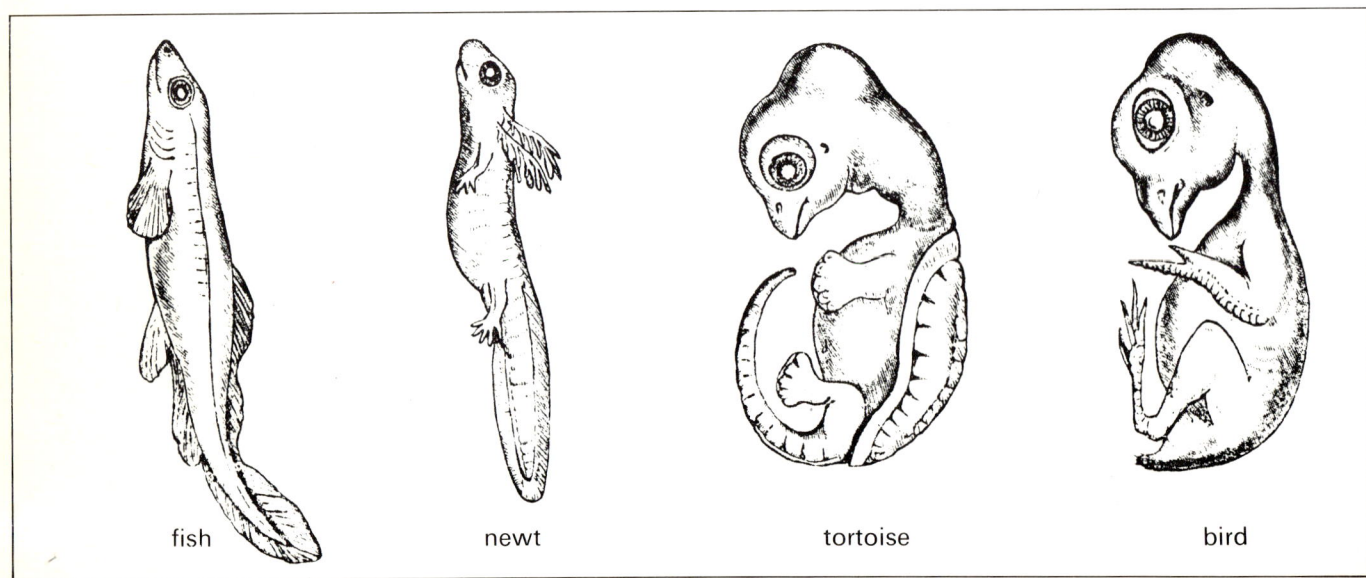

| fish | newt | tortoise | bird |

All these creatures, including humans, begin life as small fish-like embryos. To a greater or lesser extent, they repeat the whole story of evolution before they are ready to emerge into the world. First they grow gills, a tail, and the beginnings of fins from which the limbs develop. Ears form near the back of the skull. As human embryos grow, they lose their tails.

We still have traces of our origins in our bodies. The four eye teeth, or canines, were very important until apes evolved. But now they are no longer needed for seizing food.

Ears still have the remains of muscles, which once helped the ears to move into a listening position. The appendix, and the small vertebrae at the base of our spine, are relics of our evolution. We no longer need them because we have changed our way of life.

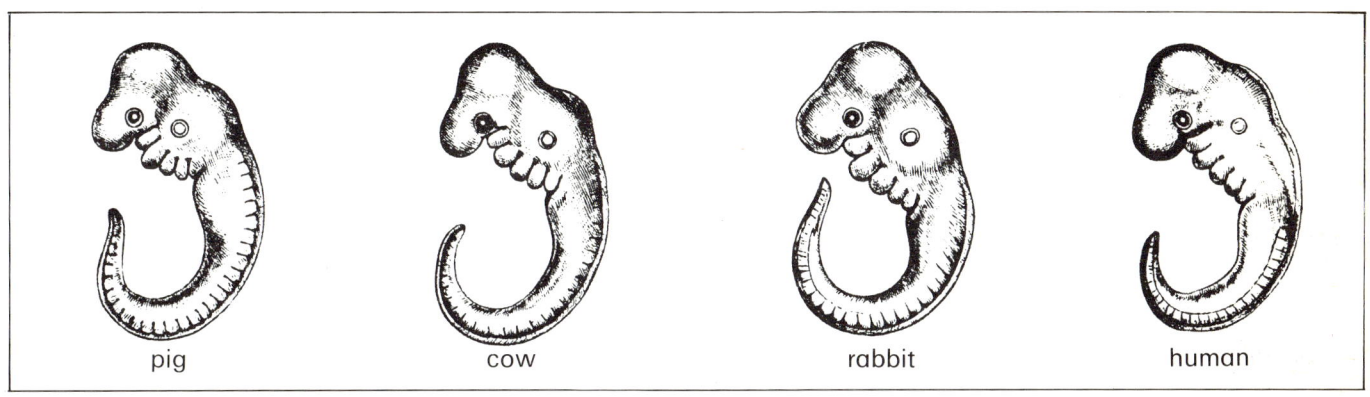

| pig | cow | rabbit | human |

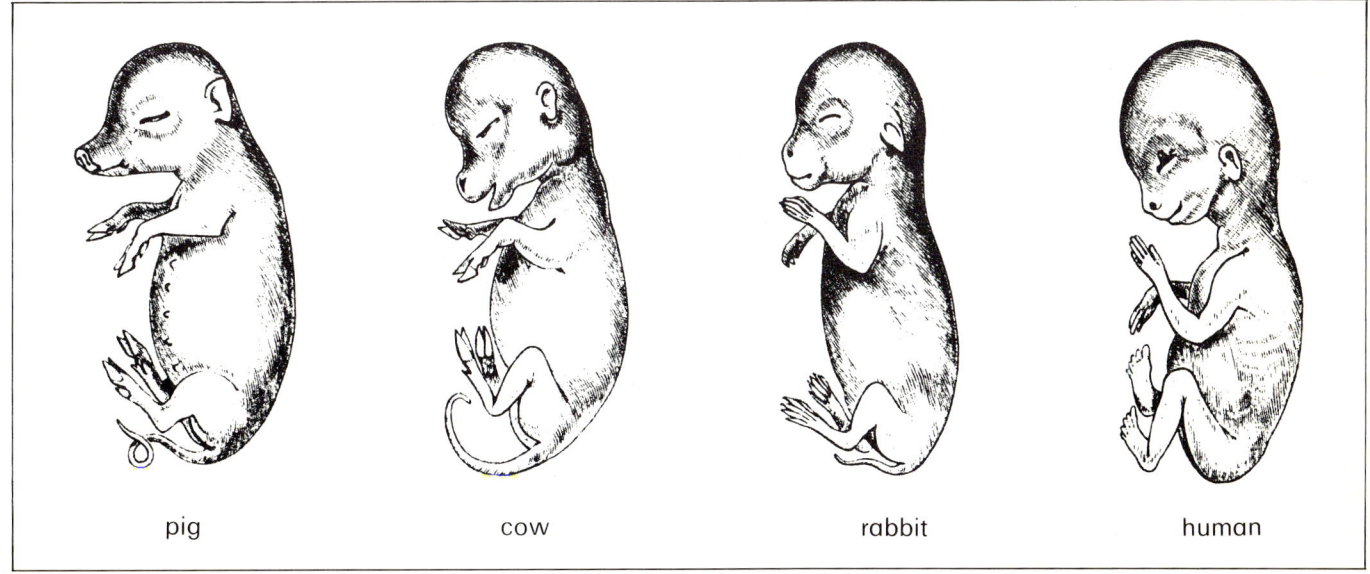

| pig | cow | rabbit | human |

apollo butterfly

ruby-tailed wasp

stag beetle

to the reptiles

early amphibian (ichthyostegalia)

insects.

solifuge

crayfish

coelacanth

crustaceans
and arachnids

early fish (or armoured fish)

invertebrates

ramshorn snail

molluscs and
cephalopods

octopus

phibians

newt

tree frog

fish

lungfish

ony fish

perch

blue shark

laginous fish

thornback ray

We have tried to make a family tree using stamps with pictures of animals. We have divided the tree into three parts. On these two pages, we will show you the evolution of fish to amphibians. The reptiles are on pages 22 and 23, and the mammals on pages 36 and 37.

The invertebrates populated the earth very early on. The left-hand 'branch' of our tree shows the three most important groups of invertebrates. At the bottom are the molluscs, in the middle the crabs and spiders, and at the top the insects.

As the sequence of embryos showed, humans can trace their descent right back to fish. You will find the main line of descent on the 'trunk' down the middle. These are the animals we shall be making out of clay and looking at more closely.

At the bottom is an early fish, the ancestor of the modern fish, as well as of all land animals. Branching off on the right are the groups which have not changed very much since they first appeared.

Sharks and rays differ from the early fish in having a flexible skeleton, made of cartilage. They do not have swim bladders. This means that they cannot float, so they have to keep moving or they will sink to the seabed.

Most fish kept the bony skeleton of the early fish and developed a swim bladder. The clumsy flippers became elegant fins.

Lungfish belong to a special class. They have gills, but they can also breathe dry air. Some close relatives of lungfish grew big fins supported by bones. This meant they could pull themselves about on the ground if their pond dried up.

These animals became the first amphibians — animals able to live in the water and on the land. Present-day amphibians include newts and frogs.

11

It all began in the water

We have made models out of clay showing the most important stages between fish and humans. The very first living things began in the water and developed there. Much later simple animals appeared in the water, and much later again, the first animals with backbones.

Susie, Claudia, Ursula and Helen have made a model of the first fish. It was plump, and had a skeleton and an armour-plated body. It probably moved very slowly, and sucked in small pieces of food from the seabed because it didn't have jaws for biting. Later fish had jaws, and pairs of fins placed behind the head and in front of the tail to help them swim.

This early fish was the ancestor of all our fish — and there are now over 25 000 kinds! Four of these — pike, perch, sturgeon and salmon — can be seen on the right at the top of the page. They all have gills which they use to take oxygen from the water.

At the bottom of the page are five water animals. They are all vertebrates, but only one is a fish. Can you guess which?

(The seal, dolphin, manatee and whale are mammals. Only the sea-horse is a fish.)

pike

chinese perch

sturgeon

salmon

monk seal

dolphin

manatee

sea horse

blue whale

13

ARCHIPEL DES COMORES

40F

RF

POSTES   CŒLACANTHE   GANDON

A walking fish

Clare and George have made a model of the fish which evolved into a four-footed land animal. It developed two organs which are needed on land — a good lung for taking oxygen from the air, and four flippers for walking.

It did not have the elegant fins we find on other fish. Instead, its fins turned into stumps strengthened with bones and muscles. They were used to prevent it rolling over when it was out of water, and to help it shuffle along on dry land. Later these stumps became the legs and feet of land animals.

Many fossils of these strange fish have been found in ancient rocks. Younger rocks don't contain these fossils, so people used to think that the fish had died out 80 million years ago. But since 1938 fishermen in the Indian Ocean have found about thirty of them. Above is a stamp from the Comoro Islands, which shows a picture of one. Its proper name is coelacanth (pronounced *seal*-a-canth).

Living on land

When Neil Armstrong landed on the moon in 1968, he took 'a giant step' for mankind. But a much bigger step was taken by the fish which left water to live on land more than 350 million years ago. They were even more awkward on land than humans are on the moon!

Things that people do almost without thinking on earth posed great problems for the first men on the moon. New ways of breathing, eating, drinking – and even speaking – had to be worked out.

In the same way, the first fish to leave the water found land strange and dangerous. They faced problems such as dryness, heat, cold and gravity. They had to adapt their bodies in order to survive.

All living things need water, because their bodies are made mainly of water. In the sea this is not a problem, but on land water is often in short supply. Every creature which stayed on land had to develop a skin which would keep in the precious water.

A few metres below the surface of the sea, the temperature stays much the same all the time. The blood temperature of most sea animals changes with the temperature of the water. The blood temperature of amphibians also varies, according to the outside temperature. They are known as cold-blooded animals.

But when cold-blooded animals are on land, they have to survive much greater changes of temperature than in the sea. In hot sun they have to stay in shady or damp places, or they will soon dry out and die.

Another problem was that of weight. Living things are almost weightless in the water. The first land animals felt the full weight of their bodies for the first time — and before their bones and muscles could support it.

The fins that became limbs helped these fish to conquer the land. They could escape from a pool when it dried up. They could also return to the water if necessary.

In the beginning they could move only a short distance over land, but slowly they learned to stay on land for longer and longer periods of time. This is how the amphibians evolved.

In less than four months, the frog repeats the evolutionary story which took nature many millions of years to complete. The frog lays its eggs in great numbers in the water. After a time tadpoles emerge, with gills and a tail.

Later on they grow legs and, after many weeks, they change into frogs. The frog has lungs, although it still keeps a moist skin which helps it to breathe. As a fully-grown frog it can live on land.

Amphibians

There are five main groups of vertebrates: fish, amphibians, reptiles, birds and mammals.

The amphibians are the smallest group, with only 2800 kinds still alive today. They live both in the water and on the land. In Europe there are two classes – tailed amphibians (which include newts) and tail-less amphibians, such as frogs and toads.

Michael and Patrick have modelled a tailed amphibian. If you were to cover its legs on both sides, you would see how closely it resembles a fish. If you are lucky and see a newt, look at the way it moves. It crawls in a wriggling way, like a fish swimming.

All amphibians have a moist skin. They also have a poisonous slime which can inflame your eyes, mouth and nose, so don't pick them up.

Frogs and toads are in great danger in our busy modern world. We fill in fishponds and pools, and so ruin their homes. When we build roads by rivers and lakes we cut them off from their spawning places. Amphibians cannot keep pace with changes in the land. They will die out if we spread ourselves everywhere, without leaving any room for them.

marbled newt

common frog

tree frog

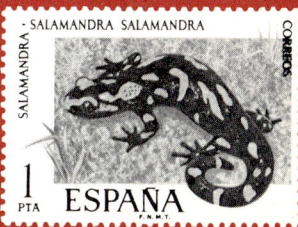

newt

midwife toad

early bird (archaeopteryx)

smooth snake

sand lizard

The ones that succeeded

Eventually, amphibians gave way to reptiles, which managed to adapt totally to life on land. Nora and Karin have made a model of a reptile. Tortoises, crocodiles, lizards and snakes are all reptiles.

Reptiles are cold-blooded, like fish and amphibians. Their skin is well protected by horny scales. A lizard can lie in wait for its prey in the sun, without drying up.

Reptiles lay their eggs in a safe place on land. The eggs are protected by a leathery skin or a hard shell. The young come out of the egg fully formed, so they are safer than young amphibians.

Reptiles once dominated the earth, sea and sky. The largest of these were the dinosaurs. The fossilised remains of one dinosaur has been found in Germany. (You can see a drawing of it at the top of the page on the left.)

This creature had jaws with teeth and a reptile's tail. But the tail also had feathers and its feet were clawed. It was one of the first birds — the ancestor of all 8600 kinds of birds on earth today.

peregrine falcon

bullfinch

mallard

firecrest

woodchat shrike

capercaillie

early bird

crocodile

grass snake

pterodactyl

tyrannosaurus

wall lizard

stegosaurus

brontosaurus

cryptocleidus

crocodiles

archosaurs   REPTILES   lizards and snakes

plesiosaurs

tortoise

brachiosaurus

tortoise

Reptiles

The middle part of our family tree shows the reptile family. In the centre you will find the reptiles still living today. The tortoises lived very early on, and they have not changed for almost 200 million years. After them the crocodiles appeared. Then came lizards and finally snakes.

On the far left we have made a collection of reptiles – strange and bizarre monsters, which have been extinct a long time. The brontosaurus was a mountain of flesh, weighing as much as ten elephants.

The two-legged tyrannosaurus was a fearsome hunter and stood as tall as a house. Stegosaurus was like a ten-tonne dragon. Its back was ridged with mighty bone plates. But all these enormous creatures had tiny brains.

To help support their great weight, some dinosaurs lived in the water. A few of their relatives even returned to the sea and developed powerful flippers. Others, like the pterodactyls, learned to fly. Some were enormous, having a wing span of about seventeen metres!

On the top of the left-hand page is one of the first birds. Its skeleton is shown on page 20.

mammal-like reptiles

Mother and child

There was a half-way stage between reptiles and mammals. Arlette and Bernadette have made a model of an animal at this stage. Unlike reptiles, mammals can keep their blood temperature roughly the same all the time. They are warm-blooded. They feed their young with milk.

When a baby lizard emerges from the egg, it doesn't need its parents. Young mammals are born helpless and need their mother's care. The young mammal has more time to prepare itself for adult life.

There are only a few mammals which do not behave like this. The duck-billed platypus lays eggs, and gives milk to the young that hatch out. The marsupials of Australia have babies that grow inside the mother, but which are very tiny when they emerge — some as small as a grain of rice. The baby then creeps into the mother's pouch where it feeds on milk and grows bigger.

Our stamp collection shows some marsupials. You will probably recognise the koala and the kangaroo.

striped possum

pen-tailed phalanger

spotted cuscus

koala

Tasmanian devil (sarcophilus)

tree kangaroo

A mouse with a future

Bruno and Roger have made a model of the first mammal. It looked like a shrew, and probably ate everything it could find, especially insects, small animals and perhaps even dinosaur eggs.

Its body was protected by fur, which helped keep it warm, even in cold regions of the earth. It was much cleverer than the dinosaurs, and able to adapt to many different habitats. All mammals living today, from mice to whales, are descended from this shrew-like creature.

Animals from the main groups or orders of mammals are shown on the stamps. Humans belong with the monkeys and apes in the order called primates. Let's take a closer look at this group.

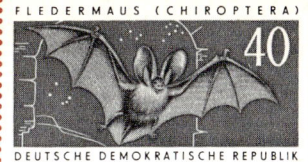

long-eared bat

african elephant

manatee

red deer

red fox

horse

red squirrel

domestic rabbit

gorilla

humpback whale

bushbaby

potto

mangabey

spider monkey

Seeing and grasping

Early on, an interesting group of tree-dwellers developed. The bushbaby and potto in our stamp collection were among the first of these. Monkeys, like the spider monkey and the mangabey, came later. They were more intelligent. Anja and Christine have modelled an early primate.

Primates live in trees. They find plenty of insects to eat, as well as fruit and birds' eggs. They have to be able to climb and jump very well, so they need good eyesight. Their eyes are at the front of their head, to enable them to focus on one point. This is vital for survival up in the treetops.

As the early primates developed, their hands, feet, and often their tail, became supple and very sensitive. With accurate sight and five clever 'hands' these tree-living animals became amazing acrobats. But they also needed a good brain to control their eyes and limbs — and so the brain began to grow.

From grasping to understanding

Some man-like apes are still alive today – for instance, the gibbon, orang-utan, chimpanzee and gorilla. Our stamps show the family life of the peace-loving gorilla.

Max and Mark have tried to model the animal from which humans and apes are descended. It had four legs, like all apes, and still lived in the trees. If it had to move along the ground it used its hands for support. Hands were used mainly for climbing and for grasping food.

It could seize a stick to reach for a fruit, or pick up a stone to drive away an enemy. But it could not make real tools or weapons. To do this, it had to have hands which were free all the time.

We can see how the eyes, hands and brain were beginning to work well together. From grasping with its hand, the primate moved on to grasping with its mind. But this primate was still a long way from being human. It needed to be able to walk on two legs, so that its hands were free. It also needed an even better brain.

30

1

2

3

4

5

1. African ape-man, *Australopithecus*, lived more than one million years ago. He walked upright and used stone tools.

2. Java ape-man *Homo erectus*, was a primitive form of human; he lived 500 000 years ago.

3. Peking man, *Homo erectus*, was another form of upright man. He mastered fire and lived from 500 000 to 300 000 years ago.

4. Neanderthal man was a skilful hunter and craftsman. He died out less than 20 000 years ago.

5. Modern man appeared about 40 000 years ago, during the end of the last Ice Age.

The ape-man was the first animal to learn to speak. It no longer relied on gestures and simple sounds, like those of a chimpanzee. It could tell its family, neighbours and fellow-hunters its thoughts and feelings through speech. Everything it learned could now be passed on to its children.

This ape-man even overcame the great fear that all animals have – the fear of fire. It learned to use fire, and to carry it about.

Early man took thousands of generations to learn all this. Walking upright, speaking, tool-making and handling fire were the skills that made the ape-man a human being.

Walking upright

Micky, Jane and Martin have made a model of the new two-legged being, together with its club and an animal it has killed. This ape-man's hands are no longer used for climbing trees or helping it to walk. They are free to try things out.

The first simple tools and weapons were made by an ape-man like this. They were kept, remembered, and improved upon.

The great inventor

Claude has made a model of a man as he lived in Europe at least 35 000 years ago. In most ways he is the same as us. Families of hunters began to shape the world into the form it is today.

If you traced your own family back far enough you would discover that this man was your ancestor. At the same time you would realise that everybody must be related to each other.

Today over 4000 million people live on earth. When this early man lived, there were only a few hundred thousand.

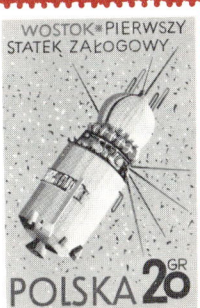
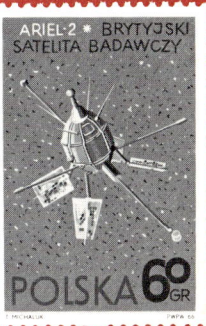

Only 20 000 years separate the first hunter and the astronaut.
Above: satellites of various nations.
Below: rock drawings of our ancestors in the Valltorta Gorge in the province of Castellon, Spain.

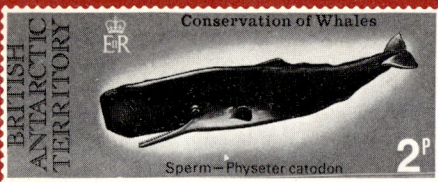
sperm whale

dormouse

man

cheetah

domestic rabbit

moose

mammals

to the primates

horse

shrew

african elephant

vampire bat

dugong

from the mammal-like reptil

chimpanzee

bushbaby

capuchin monkey

Mammals

This is the last part of our family tree. At the bottom it connects with the mammal-like reptiles. The evolution of the mammals started about 200 million years ago. Humans only appeared in the last two million years.

At the base of the tree, on the right, are the first mammals — the egg-laying duck-billed platypus, and the best-known marsupial, the kangaroo. In the centre branch is the shrew-like mammal, which lived about a hundred million years ago. All other mammals, including humans, are its descendants.

Nine of the main orders of mammals are shown on the left. At the top there is a dormouse, representing the rodents. Beside it is a whale, the largest of all mammals. This one is a sperm whale. The meat-eaters are represented by the swiftest runner, the cheetah.

There are two groups of hooved animals — those with cloven hooves, like the moose, and those with one hoof, such as the horse. The bats are the only flying mammals. This one is a vampire bat.

The mammals with trunks are represented by the African elephant. The fish-like water mammal below it is the dugong.

At the top, on the white background, are the primates — the bushbabies, monkeys, apes and man.

At the top in the middle is a human being, one of the most recently evolved creatures on earth and probably still changing, like many of the plants and animals which share the world with us.

marsupials

great grey kangaroo

duck-billed platypus

egg-laying mammals

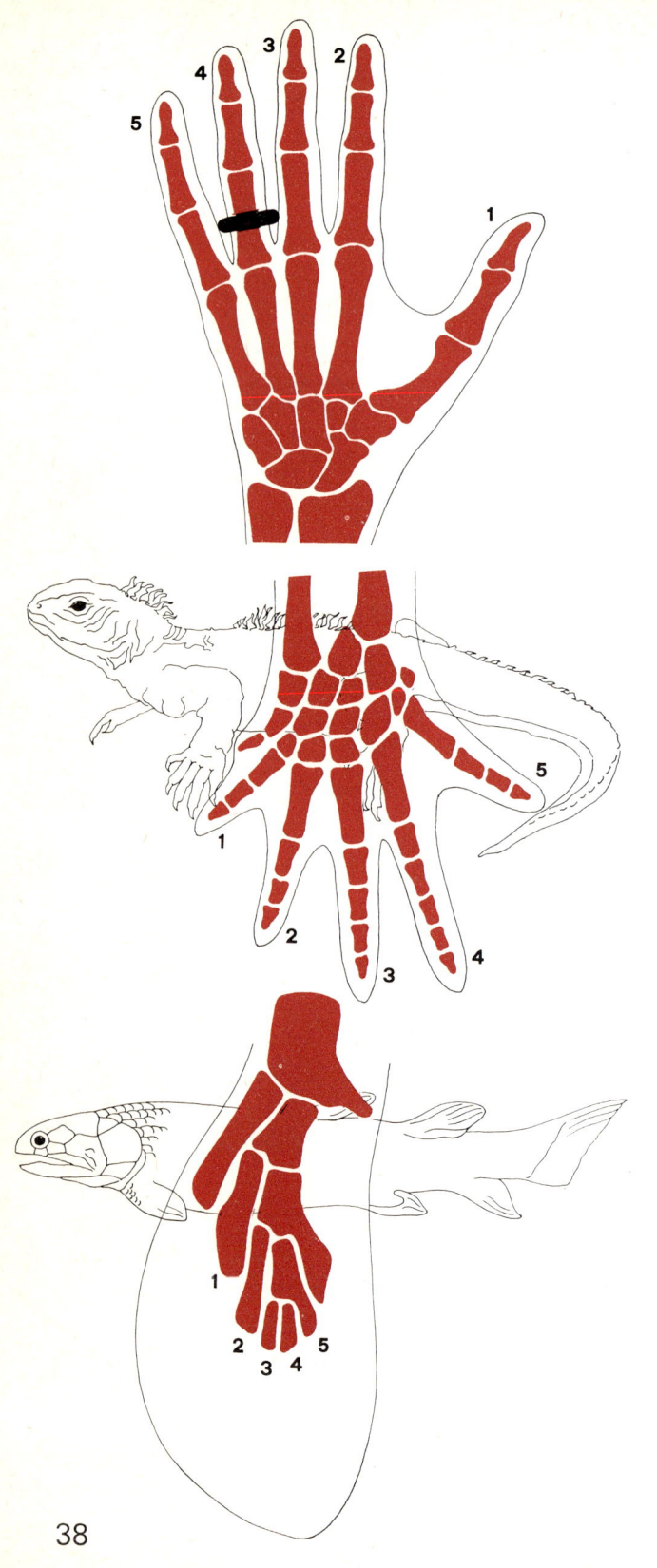

Fin ▶ paw ▶ hand

At the beginning of the book we asked a question – why is our hand like it is? We have seen that our arm and hand developed from the flipper of a fish.

The x-rayed flipper in the picture on the left at the bottom shows the beginning of our fingers. The bones are numbered one to five: 1 the thumb, 2 the forefinger, 3 the middle finger, 4 the ring finger, and 5 the little finger.

The reptile in the middle has fingers. They look different from ours.

Every mammal has the same number of bones in its fingers. Starting from the thumb, the fingers have 2, 3, 3, 3, and 3 bones. You can check this on your own hand, and in the drawing at the top.

(Solution to the puzzle on page 7. The following animals have backbones – mouse, newt, fish, bat, leopard, elephant, deer, dog, cat, crocodile, bird, lizard, horse, whale, hare.)

Suggestions for further reading

A closer look at the dawn of life (Hamish Hamilton)
Life before man, Duncan Forbes (A & C Black)
Prehistoric man, Anthony Harvey (Hamlyn)
Evolution of life, Catherine Jarman (Hamlyn)
Life through the ages, B. M. Parker (Row, Peters)
A long time ago (First interest), Robin Place (Ginn)
Dinosaurs of the earth, John Raymond (Collins)
Prehistoric animals, David Seymour (A & C Black)

More difficult books which may be useful for reference

A guide to earth history, Richard Carrington (Penguin)
History of the primates, W. E. Le Gros Clark (British Museum, Natural History)
The theory of evolution, J. Maynard Smith (Penguin)
Man and the vertebrates, A. S. Romer (Penguin)

Glossary

amphibian an animal able to live on water and on land

cartilage the firm, elastic tissue which supports some animals

class *see* classification

classification because there are so many living things, we classify them in a way which attempts to show their relationships with each other —

species:
a species is a group of plants or animals, all of the same sort. The individuals which make up the species may not all look exactly alike, but they are sufficiently similar to be able to breed together. In general, when we talk about a 'kind' of animal, we are referring to a species

genus:
a genus is a group of closely related species, often similar to look at, but not sufficiently alike for them to breed successfully. Domestic cats and wild cats belong to the same genus, but to different species

family:
closely related genera (the plural of genus) are grouped into families. Eg. the genus containing the small cats (wild cat, ocelot etc.) and the genus containing the big cats (lions, tigers, leopards etc.) are grouped together into the cat family

order:
families with similar characteristics are grouped into orders. E.g. the order carnivora includes flesh-eating mammals such as the cat family, the dog family, the weasel family, the bear family and several others

class:
orders are grouped into classes of animals. These may not look much alike, but they share basic similarities. E.g. the class mammalia includes members of the mouse order, the elephant order, the human order, the whale order and a number of others. These creatures are all warm-blooded and produce living babies which are fed on milk by their mothers

cold-blooded animal an animal whose body temperature changes according to its surroundings

embryo unborn young

family	*see* classification
fossil	the remains of a plant or animal preserved in earth
genus	*see* classification
gill	the organ which a fish uses for breathing
invertebrate	an animal without a backbone
lungfish	a fish which has lungs in addition to gills
marsupial	an animal with a pouch which it uses to carry its young
mollusc	an animal with a soft body and hard shell
order	*see* classification
primate	usually a tree-living mammal with grasping hands, forward-looking eyes and a large brain
reptile	a cold-blooded, scaly vertebrate
rodent	a gnawing mammal
species	*see* classification
swim bladder	a kind of air bladder
vertebrae	the bones which form the spine
vertebrate	an animal with a backbone
warm-blooded animal	an animal whose body temperature remains roughly constant

Index

African ape-man 32
amphibians 4, 11, 17, 19
apes 5, 27, 30, 37
ape-men 32, 33

bats 27, 37
birds 5, 6, 8, 19, 20, 22, 23
bony fish 11
brontosaurus 22, 23

cartilaginous fish 11
cheetah 37
chimpanzee 30
coelacanth 10, 14
crabs 10, 11
crocodile 7, 22, 23

dinosaurs 20, 22, 23, 27
dolphin 13
dormouse 37
duck-billed platypus 25, 37
dugong 37

elephant 7, 8, 27, 37
embryos 8–9

fish 4, 5, 11, 12, 13, 16
fire 32
fossils 14
frogs 5, 11, 17, 19

gibbon 30
gorilla 27, 30

horse 6, 27, 37

insects 7, 10, 11, 27, 28
invertebrates 4, 7, 10, 11

Java ape-man 32

kangaroo 25, 37
koala 25

language 32

lizards 4, 5, 6, 22, 23, 25
lungfish 11

mammals 4, 13, 25, 27, 36, 37, 38
manatee 13
marsupials 25, 37
modern man 9, 32, 35, 36, 37
molluscs 10, 11
monkeys 27, 28, 37
moose 37
mouse 5, 6, 8, 27

Neanderthal man 32
newt 4, 11, 19

orang-utan 30

Peking man 32
perch 11, 13
pike 13
primates 27, 28, 37
pterodactyl 22, 23

rabbit 5, 27, 36
reptiles 4, 20–3, 25, 36, 37, 38
rock drawings 35

salmon 13
satellites 35
sea-horse 13
seal 13
snails 4, 7
snakes 20, 22, 23
spiders 6, 7, 11
stegosaurus 22, 23
sturgeon 13

tortoise 8, 22, 23
tyrannosaurus 22, 23

vertebrates 7, 8, 9, 13, 19

whales 6, 13, 27, 37